Single, Saved, & Sane

The Journey of a Single Woman

All biblical references were obtained from the New King James Version

Unless otherwise stated

Editing: Pastor Shannon Robinson

Contents

IN LOVING MEMORY OF MY MOTHER

I know she would be by my side proud and celebrating, so I celebrate her. As a single woman she was a powerful influence in my life. She exemplified an independent woman who was willing to sacrifice to make a home for her children. She shared her wisdom with me and even when I didn't want to take her word, I found out that my Momma did know best!

So in her memory, I encourage you to honor and respect your mother and father and cherish their presence as you go on your journey. Rest peacefully.

Robyn L. Bibbs
July 14, 1969- January 25, 2013

Dedications

I dedicate this book to every woman who has been in a season of singleness. No matter your outcome, if you are still enduring it, have embraced it, or fighting tooth and nail, it is my hope that this book will encourage you and give you a new perspective while you wait.

To all of my friends who have laughed with me, cried with me and shared in many conversations about our lonely-selves, thank you. This is for you!

Definition

sin·gle [sing-guhl] adjective, verb, sin·gled, sin·gling, noun
adjective
1. only one in number; one only; unique; sole: a single example.
3. solitary or sole; lone: He was the single survivor.
4. unmarried: a single man.
5. *pertaining to the unmarried state*: the single life.
6. *sincere and undivided*: single devotion.

Lord, I pray that every reader of this book is encouraged and strengthened. I hope that they can gain a new perspective and hold on to the word that's received. I pray that Your grace and power will lead and guide Your women. In Jesus name I pray, Amen.

Intro

Every time I turn around there is a new deep and heart wrenching romance movie coming to the theaters or a television program to stir up the love nerves or the lack thereof. For some of us life is hard as is, and to be reminded of the missing love story in our own lives can make it even harder. I'm quite sure we all have seen one true tear jerker movie that made our heart tingle with the hope of the on screen couple making it through the devastation of life. Darn Hollywood! I don't need to be reminded of my relationship status, single!

I just want to be transparent and shed some light on this topic. Every woman's journey is unique. No two are the same. Our paths may resemble, but when we go tack for tack there are many differences. Maybe you mastered the single life and are happy as can be. Some of us find this season to be a challenge. I invite you to my experience.

Aaaaaaaaaaaaaaaaaaaaaaaaaaaaaaaaaaaaaaaaaaaaaah! That's how I feel right now. Ok, *(clears throat)*, now that I got that out of the way, let's talk. I'm going to tell you a little about me. After careful consideration, I was one who always sought out a relationship. As far as I can remember I desired and had a friend, a boyfriend or a companion of some sort. For goodness sake, I've almost gotten married twice and had some close considerations. My desire for companionship came in spurts. At one moment I would be content being alone and then the desire would return. This carried on from childhood, to my teenage years and into my adult life. I then reached a turning point and I wanted something permanent, marriage. It was no longer about satisfying my flesh for a moment, but I wanted to do things the proper and God approved way. I always had this category occupied in my life, and even with the desire for marriage, I realized I had come to a point where it couldn't be like that. I couldn't be dependent on natural companionship. I wasn't allowed to be relationship driven. As a woman striving to please God, I had a lot to learn about this area.

This season of my life was one of unfamiliarity, and discomfort, but I want to share my struggles, my victories, and my story. More power, peace and tranquility to those women who are pro-single, team-single, and their game plan is on lock.

But my truth is, being single is a battle. Being unmarried or single isn't going to take me out of the faith, but I pray continuously for God's help and contentment in my present condition.

In a picture perfect world the ideal life events are to get a diploma, land a fabulous job, meet your soul mate, get married, start a family, and live happily ever after. If only those things were easy to accomplish as listing them. Regardless of how the world says life should be designed; God has a specific design for our lives. The plan is tailored for each person, nothing duplicated. Because of this, it is imperative for us to seek God for the blueprints to our lives. If it were up to us things would go as we planned, but ultimately the plan of God will stand and trump anything we can think of.

At some point we have made life plans without the aid of God; some good, some bad, some random, some beneficial and some not too useful at all. Nevertheless, we have played a role in guiding our lives in a desired direction. I admit, before Christ I did what I wanted to do, when I wanted to and I didn't consult with anyone. So what happens to the plans we had in mind when we surrender our lives to Christ and is confronted with His preordained plans? How do we deal when things go in another direction? How do we cope with life not being life as usual? How hard or easy is it to deal when people, places, or things are taken out of our lives that we planned on keeping? Those are the things that I had to figure out.

I came to realize that although I wanted things to be a certain way in my life, it was no longer *my* way. The moment I dedicated my life to Christ I gave all authority to Him. Being in Christ means I have relinquished the control of my life and gave it over to the will of Christ. It puts me in the mind frame of being a child again. Did you ever have to ask your parent's for permission to do or get something? As a born again Christian I know to seek my heavenly father's permission and counsel when I want to do or get something. Daddy knows best. Do you also remember the time when we asked for things and didn't receive permission but still went ahead with our plans? It takes a lot to admit this, but many times we would have been better off if we would have just listened to our parents in the first place.

When it comes to dating advice, it's commonly suggested that you find the person you're interested in, or who you're compatible with, and want to begin a relationship with. And because Christian dating can be perceived as difficult and involving too many loops people may say things like, "What's the big deal, go on and jump the broom with whoever makes your heart skip a beat". But when I surrendered my life to Christ I learned that I couldn't just go and do whatever I wanted to do with who ever I wanted to whenever I wanted. I knew God had a plan and a man in mind just for me. Randi could no longer pick and choose as she pleased. With that understanding I was ready to find the mate that God had for me. I wanted to meet who I was created for.

About one year into my newly saved life, I was writing in my journal and wrote *I'm ready to be found*. I pulled that title from an infamous scripture: *He who finds a wife finds a good thing* (Proverbs 18:22).

As I began to write about waiting for my mate to find me God intervened and stopped me. Immediately I wanted to know why. What was so wrong with what I was doing? I thought it

11

was good to want to do things the right way. God impressed my heart clearly letting me know, although I was claiming to be ready to be found, I couldn't be released as a wife at the time. I put my writing on the shelf, all the while confused on why I received that type of response. I spent the next few weeks meditating on my new revelation and He uncovered the reason weeks down the line. Although I was anxious for my mate, I, as I was, was not ready at the moment. I also came to understand that if He released me at that point in time He would be replaced in my life. What did all this mean? Why wasn't I ready? There were some things, behaviors, habits, and characteristics I needed to get out of me and replaced by what He had for me. It also meant that I wasn't mature enough in God to have the balance needed to be a wife. I wasn't able to truly handle a healthy relationship with God and a man. If I had jumped into a natural relationship, it would have taken precedence in my life because I lacked a well-balanced and mature relationship spiritually. Balance comes with maturity. Balance is being able to manage and handle things properly. Balance in my situation would have been me being able to spend time with my significant friend and still know when it was time to draw back and spend time with God.

There are certain doors to be opened in our lives at appointed times. God will not allow an open door, increase or advancement in our lives until He is sure we can handle it. I simply couldn't handle it like I thought I could. And He knew it. When God said no, I could have done one of two things, receive it or reject it. We all handle what He speaks to us differently. You have the same two options when God speaks a word to your situation.

Is this the case for everyone? Maybe not, but it makes sense to me. God is the type of God that will not put us in a position to fail Him. We do that all by ourselves. When we move ahead of the plan of God we are in a position to fail Him. When we transpose the plan of God we produce things that aren't apart of the original plan. If we are honest for a moment, some of our children are due to us going ahead of the plan. It's biblical. When Abraham was waiting for the promise of God to come to pass, he moved ahead of the plan and produced a child with his concubine. That wasn't the plan of God for his life, although it

13

was similar to the plan given. If I can go deeper, some failed marriages are a result of jumping ahead of the plan of God. If we can grasp the skill of waiting for God's release it would make a world of difference in our lives.

I thank God for a teachable spirit because I am now willing to sit back and evaluate my life when instruction is given. I could have easily disobeyed those instructions and God only knows where that would have led me. I would be somewhere miserable in an un-ordained marriage wishing to get out. Who knows? God does!

I was still baffled. Why was I not ready to be released? I had all the right stuff. I wasn't too bad looking, I had a job, and a secure place of residence. I did my share of partying in my past so I was ready to settle down. Weighing all of those factors I would have been a great catch for some young man with the same ambitions. But it was this simple, I was still developing as a woman and as a woman in Christ.

Here I was, saved for a measly year and I was already trying to add another complication to my life. Not that being saved is hard, it was just a new lifestyle, new behavior, just new all the way around and I wasn't comfortable in that skin yet. Let alone trying to get comfortable with the title as someone's wife. I had to slow down and really understand what I was trying to get myself into.

What did I really know about being a wife? Was I capable of being her? Did I know what I was asking for? I had the secular mentality of being a wife. I didn't know what it was to be a Christian wife. I knew I was a down chic and I could hold the fort down in many ways, but it's more to it than that. My upbringing didn't provide me a great example of a successful marriage. Divorce and failure actually cursed my family. My mother portrayed a very independent and strong single woman, yet my grandmother was the excellent commercial housewife. Often, what we see in our surroundings is the influence of our development and that creates our identity. So I knew I wanted to handle business and be a go-getter like my mother, but provide a loving home like my grandmother. Even with just those components there were still some thing's I lacked. I was underdeveloped in the companion department. That's the part I didn't realize until after God put me on pause. I simply didn't have what it took to be released as a wife.

Five years later, I'm still learning why I wasn't ready. One thing's for certain, God does things in order and in His timing. So I am literally waiting on the Lord, as the saints would say. While I'm waiting I'm trying not to get in His way of making me who I should be, and that's a task in itself. The bible says that *he who finds a wife finds a good thing*. I want to be a good thing. Lord let me be good!

Getting worked on

God wants us to have wholeness within ourselves before we branch off and join with someone else. We can get to that point by letting God work on us and repair, restore or enhance any areas that may need it. I think it would have been unfair to my mate if I would have gone into the marriage with my brokenness. The more I come to terms with that, I begin to identify the areas of my life that need fixed week after week, and month after month. I want God to fix me privately rather than while I'm in a relationship. We should want to get all of the glitches and errors out of our lives while we are still in the workshop of singleness and before He puts us out on the shelf. I don't want to be a product of damaged goods.

As I continued to seek God on why He couldn't release me, it was revealed that as a mate we are to add too our spouse. If I am broken and a mess, I would not add, I would take from. I would take from their happiness, joy, strength, energy, and everything else that brings fulfillment. I would suck the life right out of them. Maybe you know someone like that or you are that person. You'll know by past relationships if it's you.

Have you ever done something in a relationship based off of past relationships? Have you found yourself not trusting or not forgiving someone in your life because of a past hurt or betrayal you've experienced? Have you ever done something hurtful because it was something you've done in the past? Have you reasoned within yourself that you would do things differently in your new relationship so this relationship won't end up like your last? Only for the relationship to end up worse than what you were trying to avoid? This could just be me. If we wind up in a relationship and we are a broken person, it's easy to allow our personal flaws to overtake the beauty of being in the relationship.

Relationships are beautiful, they were meant to be in the image of God; fruitful and full of life. I want to experience the fullness of one someday! Relationships prosper not void of hardship, but with hard work and a joined effort. Don't think they aren't beautiful just because some ugly things may happen, we have to work at it.

18

We can't expect a relationship to make us whole. I had to toss that mentality out of the window. Many times I found myself saying I couldn't wait until I got married so I wouldn't have this issue or that problem. But getting into a relationship wasn't going to bring a solution to the problems I had within myself. It would be adding my existing problems to a possibly good relationship. We have to strive and find wholeness before we go making ourselves available. How fun is it to try and get to know someone else if we are still trying to get to know ourselves? That needs to be accomplished before we enter into that special someone's life. My husband doesn't need me trying to discover me while we are trying to figure out how we are going to tackle life together as one. If that happens then we will not be able to live progressively.

One day I asked a friend when she was going to quit playing and get married to her longtime boyfriend. Their relationship was one of those situations when you know two people are in to each other yet they act as if they aren't. So they beat around the bush for years. Everyone knew they were destined for each other and they were just wasting time by courting. But of course we are on the outside looking in. Her response blew me away and I admired her honesty. She said, "We will get married when I become wife material". Praise God for women who can make that statement and mean it. Some of us think we are all that and a bag of chips and we are ready for a ring to be put on it. But our junk is a mess, naturally and spiritually. It takes maturity to admit that there are still some things to work on within ourselves. Don't be afraid of admitting that there are things you need to work on. The moment we acknowledge our flaws, we can get fixed.

Find your location on the scale of personal development and be honest and realistic. I do believe if men and women would examine themselves before entering relationships a lot of hearts will not get wounded. We must find a place of honesty. Because I was so young when I began my so called "dating" I had a premature understanding of what it meant to be in a relationship. And simply because I didn't know it caused me to have un-healthy and un-prosperous relationships. Unfortunately I didn't get the sit down talks with my parents about how it was to have a crush, have a boyfriend, or what it was like to fall in love.

Values and expectations weren't instilled into me. So it was easy for me to give my heart away every chance it seemed like a good idea. What I am about to say may seem like an excuse to some people and that's ok, but this is what I know for a fact in my life. A missing link in my development was caused by not having a father figure in my life growing up. I sought after acceptance, recognition and love from male figures because I didn't know what it was like to have a man love me. I now know I was only receiving Eros love and not Agape love. I believe a lot of us women have been there. Many will continue to argue if that's just a lifelong excuse, but it does play a major role in our development. At some point we have to rise out of that cursed excuse and live.

There are many qualities that the virtuous wife possess and I am sure those didn't come overnight. In your own time think about what makes up a good woman and a good wife? And ask yourself if you possess some of those qualities?

Proverbs 31:10-31 Who can find a good wife? For she is worth far more than rubies that make one rich. The heart of her husband trusts in her, and he will never stop getting good things.

21

She does him good and not bad all the days of her life. She looks for wool and flax, and works with willing hands. She is like ships that trade. She brings her food from far away. She rises while it is still night and makes food for all those in her house. She gives work for the young women to do. She gives careful thought to a field and buys it. She plants grape-vines from what she has earned. She makes herself ready with strength, and makes her arms strong. She sees that what she has earned is good. Her lamp does not go out at night. She puts her hands to the wheel to make cloth. She opens her hand to the poor, and holds out her hands to those in need. She is not afraid of the snow for those in her house, for all of them are dressed in red. She makes coverings for herself. Her clothes are linen cloth and purple. Her husband is known in the gates, when he sits among the leaders of the land. She makes linen clothes and sells them. She brings belts to those who trade. Her clothes are strength and honor. She is full of joy about the future. She opens her mouth with wisdom. The teaching of kindness is on her tongue. She looks well to the ways of those in her house, and does not eat the bread of doing nothing. Her children rise up and honor her. Her husband does also, and he praises her, saying: Many daughters have done well, but you have done better than all of them. Pleasing ways lie and beauty comes to nothing, but a woman who fears the Lord will be praised. Give her the fruit of her hands, and let her works praise her in the gates.

Insane in the Membrane

To be sane is to have good sense! As a single person we have to have good sense, period. We need to have a clear and balanced mind as well as good sight and hearing, naturally and spiritually when it comes to relationships.

I'm sure when you read the title you may have wondered why would sanity be tied into this topic. So here is the reason why: If you're anything like me, when the time clock of life is ticking away and you haven't quite reached some milestones you expected, you can slowly begin to toss good and common sense out of the window. There have been times where I've snapped out of a funk and thought to myself, *"Wow Randi, you're acting like you don't have any sense"*. When we get impatient, we can begin to act out of character. Meaning some things can become acceptable that once wasn't. Standards can begin to be lowered and compromise seems a little more appealing. So my title is to brag a little bit and say that we are single beautiful women, who are saved by grace through faith, and we are in our right mind!

We have made it this far and haven't jumped on the looney wagon or onto a burning train of fleshly destruction.

Now I can only talk for myself. Being a person who was accustomed to the dating game since an early age, hitting a single season in my life was like hitting black ice. It was dangerous and unexpected and I wanted to get off of it rather quickly, yet safely. I had a lot to learn during this time. It took this season to make me realize that God never said that I would get married, that was my plan. Maybe He spoke that to you, but the first assignment given to His creation, Adam, was to dress and keep the responsibility given to him (Genesis 2:15). His mate came after those instructions. I needed to learn how to deal with this unfamiliar place and since I didn't know how long I would be single I needed to learn how to trust that God was going to keep my mind sane. I was used to making my own choices and planning my next move, but I was submitted to God's plan for my life.

As women of faith Christ has to be first in our lives. Moment of truth; I have found it easy to make the mistake of putting natural relationships before my spiritual relationship. We

24

have to grow to the point where He can trust us to add another person into our lives without Him getting tossed to the back burner. If you forget about God just because you are dating, then you better check yourself. I know from experience God will shut all things down that's unlike Him if and when they get in the way. We can make our relationships our god when we seek them more than God, our Creator. They become an idol in our life and we know how God feels about idolaters.

Exodus 20:2-5 "I am the LORD your God, who brought you out of the land of Egypt, out of the house of bondage. You shall have no other gods before Me. You shall not make for yourself a carved image--any likeness of anything that is in heaven above, or that is in the earth beneath, or that is in the water under the earth; you shall not bow down to them nor serve them. For I, the LORD your God, am a jealous God".

It's common to hear of people searching for a spouse once they get saved instead of seeking God. Of course marriage is the proper thing to do if you want to be with a person and enjoy life as one. But there are some who only do it to live a life free from sexual sin. Yes of course we want to be without sin, but don't rush to get a mate for that reason alone. Getting married doesn't make life easier; it actually draws more attacks to you spiritually because satan is against Godly unions. So hold on to your socks! Two is always better than one, especially in the Kingdom of God. Getting married doesn't prevent other temptations. It gives us a license to be intimate with another person, but we still have to practice self-control. Do not allow sex to persuade you to jump the broom. Think past the honeymoon! We will be better off asking God for strength and power to remain abstinent until our time comes and something shifts! We must desire to be righteous before God, period. If we aren't right before the ring how do we expect to be after? A shiny diamond will not change our lack of self-control. So be sure to keep your mind at ease and stayed upon God as you fight the fight of staying pure.

There was so much that God wanted to show and teach me in my singleness but I wasn't looking at it that way. Being single is an advantage because of the alone and personal time we can have with the Lord. I began to limit God the moment my focus was placed on something else. I've come to know that the enemy is crafty in his attacks. He tries to find ways to get us caught up. His ultimate goal is to get us to turn our backs on God and quit. Even when we think we are sure in our faith he will still try his hardest to get us. And with his many of attacks, he may not be able to get us to sin but he can cause us to become distracted. Or what if he is able to get us to sin? He'll try to keep us in a low position so we won't have enough strength to try to get out. If and when we get through the testing he'll let up for a season, but remember, ultimately he wants to take us out, so he will be back!

I preached a message once called "It can't stop and it won't stop". In that message I brought attention to the fact that when we are on the right path with God and walking in His plan here comes satan and his old sneaky self trying to trip us up and out of the will of God. But we have to be determined and ahead of the game to see the devices that he's trying to throw our way. When I understood the attack that was on my life I was determined to recognize satan's schemes and devices. I began to notice a pattern. It was usually when I was on the brink of God moving on my behalf or after I had a good season of being focused on God that out of nowhere appears a mystery man in my face. At first I was oblivious to it, but then I really seen the pattern. Then I realized that the longer I respond the same way to each attack and get set back, the longer it was going to be before the real deal can happen. When we respond differently to satan's attack, he no longer has us figured out. I'm being played the fool when I walk right into the trap. The trap sometimes does look mighty fine. Sometimes the trap has a *Jesus* tag on it. Sometimes the trap will be the very thing that I am looking for but don't need. Satan plays on our lustful desires. The bible says that we are drawn away and enticed by our own lusts. We fall away and off into la la land because *we* want to. Let's be honest. The bait was thrown, we bit and now we are somewhere swimming in the ocean and stuck! But thanks be to God that we are never too far from His help. God doesn't tempt us. The bible is very clear and you may know from experience that God can lead us to a place of temptation but not to fail Him. He leads us there to overcome and prove that we can be victorious over our flesh. The enemy wins every time we give over to our flesh. Take a moment to give God thanks for not dealing with us according to what our sins deserve.

Do you notice any patterns in your life? Have you been a repeat offender? It's ok to tell the truth, God already knows the answer, do you? I mean seriously, once I caught on I was like oh silly devil, you won't win again. I'm growing up out of this issue. I mean the attacks were so consistent in manner that one day I remember breaking it off with a guy and literally the very same day a friend from high school contacted me on a social media site. At first I was thinking wow, I haven't heard from them in a long time, so we began to chat. But the moment I started to feel those old feelings rise my Holy Ghost flag started waving. After I paused for a minute I thought, what a coincidence this brotha comes telling me he's been thinking about me and wants to get reunited right when I was ending a previous relationship. So here I was freeing myself from one distraction to get back on track with God, and satan wanted me to walk right back into another distraction. This revolving door was all an attempt to keep me away from my relationship with God. Tisk, tisk devil, I got you figured out. I'm keeping my mind stayed upon God.

Seeking Him

There's a demonstration that my Pastor does about seeking God first. It shows that when we keep our eyes on the stuff, callings, houses, mates, cars, etc.), rather than on God we are unable to see God. But when our eyes are on God we are not only able to see our stuff but able to get the stuff also. The stuff represents everything He has for us and things we desire that are outside of Him. Sometimes it's not that we aren't allowed to have things, we just have to wait for the stuff to be given in His timing. Trying to understand His timing versus our timing is a mystery. I say it's almost impossible to understand, that's why we have faith. Faith calms our impatience and settles our frustrations when they flare up. Faith tells me that maybe He has something better for me. Faith gives me a new perspective and challenges my outlook on life. Faith says *what if my mate isn't ready for me, as I may be for him*? This is why it's very important to seek God about what concerns you.

Seeking God is very beneficial no matter who you are, single, married or widowed. In my book *A Closed Mouth Don't Get Fed*, I discuss the purpose and power that come from prayer.

When we go before God in prayer about our natural connections, which we should be doing, He directs us. His word is a lamp to our feet and a light to our path. The word is not only the readable word of God but the word He speaks to us personally. If you haven't sought God about who you should be connected to you may want to reconsider and do so. Apply this principle to all associations.

Some of us are guilty of going to our friends and asking their opinion on someone we want to date. We should be just as quick to do that with God. He knows more about these people than any other person would. He has the ability to enlighten us on some things better than our gossiping girlfriend. Let's go deeper. He has the ability to tell us some things that person wouldn't even tell us. God can tell you if Mr. Fine-Chocolate is an abuser or that Mr. Has-it-all doesn't have your best interest in mind. There are some wolves in sheep's clothing and we can be so mesmerized that we neglect to see what God is really saying about them. God can reveal the red flags and give the green lights and when He does we have to know when to follow His lead. Do not ignore the revealed signs, especially when they are given from the Lord, He's always right. Trust that His "No" is because He "Knows". Don't get upset if God is constantly telling you no in regards to who you let into your life. Take those instructions as precious treasures. He is only protecting you, keeping you, and saving you for something greater. I understand that too many no's from the Lord can sure be discouraging. But I'd rather accept a no from God than live a life of regret, wouldn't you?

What does the written word say to us about connections? It instructs to not be unequally yoked. What communion does a believer have with a non-believer? The New Living translation says,

"Don't team up with those who are unbelievers. How can righteousness be a partner with wickedness? How can light live with darkness"?

This scripture doesn't mean it's only the unsaved people outside of the church. We can be unequal and in the church together holding hands and singing hymns. You can be unequally yoked simply because you're on different levels. Have you ever tried to have a spiritual conversation with a carnal person? It may not go too well because they aren't interested in the things that you are. When I first got saved the guy that I was head-over-heels in love with invited me over for a nice evening. Side note: this moment is how I knew my life was changed by God and it was only the beginning of my tests! I told him that I would come over but I was going to talk about God the entire time. Without hesitation he told me never mind. You see we weren't speaking the same language anymore. I was a new creature so I no longer had the desire to do what I used to do. He wanted my company until I told him that my conversation was changed. Some would have gone over there and gave in to the flesh. But when you have truly been changed, you can take a stand for God and He will back you up!

The bible also says to not be deceived, evil communication corrupts good manner. Why would it say "do not be deceived"? There are going to be some situations that have all the qualities of being an ok thing, but we must read between the lines and not be afraid to separate ourselves from what's not good for us. I know that was your bestie and you shared lots of laughs together, but your reputation and purity should be most important.

We need healthy and ordained relationships and that is produced by two individuals who are on the same track. It's normal for the good girl to be attracted to the bad boy, and in the end the girl turns bad. So we have to change that contagious effect and become un-persuadable. Take a stand for Christ and never compromise. What looks and sounds good is not always good for us. We serve a God who won't withhold any good thing from us, so you will not be missing out on anything that God can't supersede!

Ladies lets not seek out the lowercase him, but rather the greater Him and everything else will happen in its time. When we seek the *him* we look for all of the wrong things. Our decisions are made upon the wrong factors. We will fall for the wrong guy but say it's ok as long as he has a job, car, a house and can dress nice. As long as he puts a ring on it, we're cool, but he's a liar, thief, womanizer, and the incredible hulk behind closed doors. If you have a case where everyone is against the person you are interested in, do not think everyone is hating on you! Sometimes our friends and family members are able to see what we can't or refuse to see. Grandma or Sista Matty may say,

"Child I don't know about him." She is not telling you that because she wants him, she may have a revelation that he ain't no good for your life.

Our gut feelings at times are very truthful. If you are unsure or you can't hear from God, be sure to seek counsel when it comes to major decisions in your life. If we follow those and not get so blinded by love or the fact that we have to have a man, we can save ourselves from a lot of heartache.

Occupy until He comes

It is my dream to get married one day; nevertheless, I have to be ok with the possibility of my mate not coming for another one, five, or seventeen years. Lord Jesus! Let's be rational and eliminate our projected timeframe. What if God decide it's not His will for you to have a mate but to serve Him only? What would you do, would you be ok? Do you kick against the pricks and go get you a man? After I evaluated the results of my attempts at relationships, I took those as clear signs of God saying, "not yet Randi". And because I knew that I forfeited my power over my life decisions, I had no choice but to submit to His plan.

We have to be ok with God's plan being different than our expectations or previous plans. After we receive His guidance and instruction will we live a life of frustration, disappointment, dissatisfaction, or bitterness? Or will we make the best of the situation, swallow all self-made plans and live satisfied? I choose a life satisfied by the will of God.

We have to occupy until he comes. Occupy is to take or fill up (space, time, etc.) or to engage or employ the mind, energy, or attention of. This is twofold, we have work to do for God until He returns for us and we have to work until he, our mate comes. We can't sit around and let precious time pass us by. There is a divine assignment that each person is given and we can't sit around neglecting our assignment just because we don't have a mate. Us fulfilling God's will is not contingent upon our marital status. We have to work while we can until either Jesus comes back for us or our mate comes, and then when he comes, we still have to keep working. Occupy until he comes.

Before you were formed God knew you would be right where you are. He also knew He had a work for you to accomplish during this time. It's in your time of solitude that you can work to your fullest capacity without strain because your attention is undivided. Have you ever wandered off into worship or studying the word of God into the midnight hours? Or have you been able to participate in ministry or go out with the ladies and enjoy the night? There's so much to explore in the Lord while we are single.

Paul gave us his opinion on the topic of marriage.

1 Corinthians 7:8-9 *But I say to the unmarried and to the widows: It is good for them if they remain even as I am; but if they cannot exercise self-control, let them marry. For it is better to marry than to burn [with passion].*

And then goes on to say in verses 32-33

"But I want you to be without care. He who is unmarried cares for the things of the Lord--how he may please the Lord. But he who is married cares about the things of the world--how he may please [his] wife".

When we get into a relationship we have to talk to that person, spend time with them, cook, take care of ourselves, take phone calls, enjoy nights out on the town, entertain company, and a million other things and still manage to get in the word, seek the face of God and be sure to hear His voice. I believe Paul evaluated both ends of the playing field and came to the conclusion that singlehood is where it is!

He's not saying it's a sin to fall in love and get married, he is stating that our focus and energy would be shared between two. When you are married you have to juggle how you're going to take care of home, your spouse and maintain pleasing the Lord. So his personal suggestion is if you can, remain single as he was. If you are a person who is blessed enough to stay single and be content, then do that. Live your single life to the fullest walking out your God given gift. Paul was determined to fulfill the will of God and we should desire to imitate that very same determination.

Find something to do until he comes. We spend so much time trying not to be single that we forget to live as a single. Live! Explore! Laugh! Cry. Find out what extra-curricular activities you enjoy doing. Take up a hobby. Challenge yourself to accomplish a goal. Set out to become the best woman you can be. Get restless doing your dream. Dance. Shout! Get to work and then go to sleep, wake up and do it all over again. Find fulfillment in yourself until he comes and then welcome him into your life and he can enjoy it with you. Start this today!

Oops!

Once you have confessed the words, I do, there is no taking it back. We can not make permanent decisions with temporary feelings. Some mistakes can be an easy fix. Oops, sorry I ordered the wrong item or I signed my name wrong. But when vows are involved things are 100% real. We can not wake up one day and say, "Oh I'm sorry I didn't mean to marry you." Marriage is a serious matter.

Women are emotional creatures. Sometimes we make decisions because of how we feel at the moment. Eve, the first woman created, felt like she was missing out on something she never knew of so she allowed her emotion of curiosity to kill her spiritually. Our emotions can get us in trouble! I have made some choices in my life because it felt right. I have ignored logic and skipped-to-my-lu on down to la-la land because it "seemed" right. Boy oh boy, there is a way that seems right to man, but in the end is the ways of death. *A spiritual death that is.*

One time I was counting down the months to my scheduled wedding day. I began to notice that my fiancée and I disagreed on some things, yet we were supposed to be getting closer to one another during this time. The flags were waving because this was serious, it involved my future. If we were going to spend the rest of our lives together there shouldn't be any secrets or surprises to be revealed after the wedding day. Oh no my brotha, lets iron these things out before I meet you at the altar in my white dress. Now let me explain because of course all relationships will have disagreements. It doesn't matter how great and perfect you think your relationship is disagreements are unavoidable.

It is ok to disagree, some disagreements are healthy disagreements. Our case of disagreements was about key issues such as honest communication. Communication is crucial for the success or failure of a relationship. It's proven to be one of the top reasons why relationships fail. When two people are preparing to join together in a lifelong commitment certain things shouldn't be hidden from one another. You should be able to share your vision and goals, where you see each other in five years, and blah-zay-blah. There should simply be no secrets. One day in conversation my fiancé told me that he wasn't going to tell me his life vision until after we got married. Again, I could have been ok with that if I was naive and believed that God would have me walking into a door blinded. For all I knew he could have had plans to take me away to Zimbabwe and made us serve a golden elephant in twenty years. Side note: when we marry, we are to submit to our husband's lead. Therefore, if I would have gotten married and my husband's decision was to move to another state, I would have to follow his lead as a humble wife because of the declaration, till death do us part. Know the facts before you say I do. It may prevent a lot of surprises.

When he told me his stance, I had two options before me. One was to ignore the warning flags and submit to a man knowing that there could be more things revealed that I didn't agree with. Two was to take the signs as a way of escape and politely cancel the plans and prayerfully get over the let-down of not becoming who I thought I was, a wife. I could have been stuck on the fact that it was really about to happen. I had started purchasing decorations, planning our invites, and I even placed the down payment on my gown. I had everything ready, but God!

The more I thought about what I was getting myself into and what I had done to get to that point; I realized that I didn't really seek God on what His thoughts were about the marriage arrangement in the first place. I was going along with the plans because things felt right and a few people encouraged me in it, everything *felt* ok. Of course things were going to feel ok to me because I never asked the source was it ok.

I didn't call the wedding off just yet, but it was on thin ice. A little more time went by and we had another disagreement and that was the final straw! I called my best friend and told them the wedding was off. Thank God I was discreet with my dealings in the first place because not many people knew about the marriage plans. Side note to those who like to share your personal life with others, if you keep your business out of everyone's minds it won't be in their mouths. My friend encouraged me to pray about it before I made any quick decisions. Those instructions only confirmed how I failed to pray about this in the beginning. God may not always speak to us when we want Him to, but He will when we need Him to. The very next Monday evening I attended a leadership prayer session and I knew I really needed direction because I was frustrated about my situation. I prayed that He would show me the way. Let me tell you that I left that night with a new understanding of my situation. The people who we connect ourselves too always serve a purpose. Needless to say, I wasn't getting married that fall, but I was confident that our connection was not in vain. We both walked away with valuable lessons learned and I do not regret any second of it. Some may think that I was foolish to walk away from an opportunity to say that I am someone's wife, but I say it was wisdom that spared my life. Never make a commitment out of obligation. The only person you owe your life to is God.

Marriage is a serious matter and should be handled as such. When you are considering someone to be your mate and even when you are making the wedding plans, be sure that your feelings isn't just a phase. There is no such thing as love at first sight and married the next night. Marriage is a spiritual and natural investment that can reap great benefits to those who do it the right way.

I won't settle

A new year rolled around and not much had changed in my life. More days, weeks, and months had gone by and there were still no signs of a serious relationship or marriage in my near future. Friends of mine were getting boo'd up and preparing for weddings, while I still sat on the sideline congratulating. The issue wasn't me not being able to get a date; I could have been in a relationship without a problem. But I refused to let loneliness get the best of me. I didn't want to settle for any man. My friend jokingly said that when women get lonely we'll take that man, her man, any man, Lord give us Pac Man! I cracked up laughing because sometimes that's true! Just to get a date we will go out with the one who's willing to treat us. We will go out with someone knowing deep down inside we have no interest in them whatsoever, but just because we're tired of sitting at home on a Friday night we are willing to test the waters.

This goes back walking in the plan of God. Walking in the plan of God a lot of times involves waiting, trusting, and depending on His direction. We have to know that we are no longer our own. I can no longer do what I want to do without the consent and approval of my Heavenly Father, or I'll pay the price if I'm disobedient by not waiting, trusting, and depending on His direction. When our focus is more on the length of our singleness we have to stay guarded because compromise, lowering of standards, settling and whispers can come to pay us a visit.

I remember hitting a point where I was becoming restless from waiting and a certain someone was coming around me more frequently. Again it felt okay. I guess I was expecting God to jump down from Heaven to forbid me to have a conversation with this person if it was wrong. Since He didn't, I took it as me not getting a clear yes and I wasn't a clear no either. So maybe it was ok to pursue a cordial relationship with this person again. This person was someone I had dealings with years back and at one point we tried to take things further but it was shut down. I now know that it was shut down because at that particular time in my life God had other plans for me and a relationship would have been a distraction to my growth in God. I had to believe that I wasn't being denied because I didn't deserve it, I was denied because He wanted to get me to Himself and mold me into a mature believer before I entertained the thought of a natural relationship.

I thought this was love coming back around in perfect timing because a few years had gone by since our last encounter. The more he came around feelings began to revisit and thoughts of what we could be together again developed. Again I was instructed to seek God for direction. I didn't want this time to be like the last, when I went by my feelings and failed to seek the counsel of God. God has our best interest in mind and we have to be confident in that. When I went to pray I was thinking to myself here it goes, it was all or nothing. This was the second time that I genuinely went before the Lord about a relationship. I was never the person who prayed for natural things. I wanted wisdom, power and revelation. I was seeking for the things that man couldn't give me.

I asked God what should I do about this situation, did He approve of it, what should be my next move because right then and there I didn't know what to do. Everything seemed ok, we had a good vibe and great communication again. I could see the potential in the relationship and I could also see some of the benefits. But God knew how serious me getting an answer was because His response was undeniably understood. As clear as a summer sky I felt in my spirit, "the moment you say yes you will be settling and missing out on what I have for you." I think my heart stopped for two point five seconds after that; first, because He spoke to my heart clearly and secondly, because He cared enough about me to address a petition that I brought to Him. I was in awe. Do you believe that God speaks? He does. To this very day I hold on to that word. It keeps me when I feel like settling. That word encourages me when I feel like giving up. I'm pushed to wait for a release because of that word.

When God speaks to us concerning what we are concerned about take heed to those words. He said if I would have said yes, if I had put myself in agreement with that person, if I decided to walk into a relationship with that person, I would be settling. Do you know what it means to settle? To settle is to be satisfied with something as is. That's like me saying I want to sell my car. It's worth five thousand dollars, but if you buy it today I'll settle for two. No, no, no! I want all of my profit! I want everything that God has for me. God made it clear to me that I would miss out on what He has if I accepted that person right then and there. I have hope and expectancy even more than before. That word tells me that there is someone better than what I was thinking was good at that moment. I don't want what's good, I want what's God and that will be great! On the flip side, because I don't want you to think that just because God says no to a person in their current condition that doesn't mean it still couldn't be that person. He could have meant he wasn't right for me at that particular time, that day, that season of his life. What if he hadn't reached his fullest potential in Christ? What if God wanted to clean and fix him up to be the ordained mate for me and accepting him as he was would have stunted his growth? That's something to think about huh? Now I really have to wait and see.

Here's some icing to this cake. When God speaks do we have the faith and boldness to listen and obey? Does it matter how much you have invested into a relationship or how high your expectations are to stay or leave if God said so? Can you pull out your chips in hopes of avoiding a major loss or set back?

I'd rather count the cost and say goodbye than deal with the consequences of displeasing God. I want my first marriage to be my last marriage!

After receiving those convicting words from God I was ok for a while. I didn't even want to think twice about that person. You see what the enemy likes to do is come behind God and plant seeds of doubt and curiosity. After we receive a word he'll try to get us to question what we've heard and know to be true. *Did He say you couldn't eat from every tree?* And then we get to asking, well did He? If God says no, don't start doubting or questioning Him. Don't think you misunderstood. Take Him at His word.

Just in case you are unsure of God's word, he is so awesome that He will do things like send other messengers and reminders to confirm the word spoken to us. It's refreshing to get a friendly reminder some days. Not too long after my answered prayer I started preparing a message for the homeless shelter that my church outreach ministers at. I was encouraged by the story of Hannah in the bible and I began to feel Him tell me that waiting on Him was beneficial. Also I felt that during this wait I would receive more strength. I was going to receive more strength because the wait could possibly be longer than I anticipated. Around this same time our church held a prayer conference and the original scheduled speaker had an emergency at home which prevented her from speaking so another speaker was called in to take her place. The service was going on as planned and after praise and worship my grandmother said she had a word for me. I was shocked because she had never given me a word my entire life. When the service began to close out the minister began to operate in the prophetic. She began to call people up and tell them what God was saying. Me being me, I wasn't expecting to get a word because I usually never do when a prophet comes to visit the church. So the minister gets to me and says a few things about my role in the ministry and spirit. Then she began to hit the sensitive spot, she told me that God was preparing the man to stand up tall beside me and some other stuff that I can't seem to remember. The service ended and as I was walking my grandmother to her car I asked her what she was going to say to me. She replied, "She already said it", referring to the prophecy. She said, "God told me to tell you to wait. That special someone is coming, just wait."

I said all of that to say that God will send confirming messages and reminders to us when He wants us to hold on to His word and His will. My word was to wait. Anything outside of that will be against the will of God.

What has God spoken to you concerning your life?

You'll get what you ask for

While we wait and seek God for His will to be done in our lives we have to be very careful with our seeking and asking. The bible informs us that if we delight ourselves in the Lord He will give us the desires of our hearts and it instructs us to seek the Kingdom of God first and *things* will be added to us. Those two passages are important for us who wait. If and when we seek the Kingdom of God first, our focusing is not on the stuff. Remember that stuff I mentioned before? Our mate could fall in the category of stuff to be added.

Seeking the Kingdom first also reduces the specific demand of a thing. It keeps our prayers on a level of *Lord have Your way in my life. Fulfill the plans that You have for me. Remove and place whoever You desire in my life* and so forth. Rather than, *God I want my husband to be honey-nut brown complected, with silky-smooth skin, muscles, a new car, and flawless credit.* If we seek God first He will be sure that all the things we desire are all inclusive. Better yet He will make sure that he has everything we need and sometimes our needs do not match our wants. I'm sure He will even throw in some extras for us.

A mistake we can make is to keep asking for something that God doesn't intend on giving us. You know the saying "be careful of what you ask for because you might just get it"? We need to really consider that saying. We can be so caught up in asking for a relationship, a marriage, a particular person or type that even if it goes against the plan of God, He will give us just what we continue to ask for. Even when it doesn't seem like it, there are good reasons behind God saying no and not yet. You know how it is when your parent threatened you not to ask why they have said no! I know that has happened to me. When a parent gives a response that's it, it's settled. Case closed.

We have to be sensitive enough to believe God even when we don't necessarily know why He has given instruction, direction or said certain things to us.

In the bible the children of Israel wanted to be like the other nations and have a King rule over them although it was God's plan for them to be lead by Him. Can you see where I am going? God sent a warning to the children of Israel about how life would be with this King they wanted so badly, and they still demanded a King despite the preview. At their request, they got what they asked for.

> 1 Samuel 8:19-22 *But the people refused to listen to Samuel's warning. "Even so, we still want a king," they said. We want to be like the nations around us. Our king will judge us and lead us into battle. So Samuel repeated to the LORD what the people had said, and the LORD replied, "Do as they say, and give them a king."*

If you are not familiar with this passage you would think it was a good thing that God granted their request. But it turned out being the worst thing they could have ever asked for. The moral of the story is, we have to be very careful about what we ask, plead, and beg God for, because we just might get it. There is a method to God's madness. He is all knowing and we can't think that we know it all either. Two know-it-alls will clash every time. Just think about that person you know that has the answer for everything! Do you find yourself frustrated because their amazing, un-humanlike knowledge of all things is just out of this world? God knows best. His ways are higher than ours and He has seen the end of our life before the beginning. So it's pretty safe to say that He knows what He's doing a little better than we do.

Whenever I'm feeling anxious for my mate or anything for that matter, I seek God about it. If no results or answers come my way, I encourage myself. How? By remembering that God knows how much I can bear. He knows how long we can handle being alone. He knows how long we need to be alone. I may be ready to pull my hair out, but He knows it all. Just because we may not know doesn't mean that He doesn't. God is better at managing your life than you think He is not! With that understanding we have to learn to be ok in our season of singleness.

God displays His strength to the fullest in our moments of weakness. He's the master at pulling us out right at the time of need. When Adam was alone in the Garden of Eden, at a certain point God said that it was not good anymore. Whatever was going on with Adam at that moment, God seen it, He knew it, and said "Oh no my brotha, I need to bring someone your way". Adam had no choice but to trust God's judgment. When you think about it that's all he could do. God only created him and placed him in a fully equipped, furnished, and all-expense paid place. All the hard work was already done. So all Adam knew to be was submissive to the plan of God. God caused Adam to sleep and He pulled a rib out of him to create Eve, bone of his bone and flesh of his flesh. God pulled her out, put them together and blessed them. He said be fruitful and multiply. Be encouraged, He knows what you need and when you need it. The next time you feel uneasy or discouraged just tell yourself that your mate is sleeping right now. Even when you feel like you are ready, he may not be. God will pull you out when the time is right!

Keep it up

Once we are blessed to get into a relationship we have to always be conscious of our relationship status with Christ. When we go changing our social media relationship status to dating, taken, and married, make sure our status with Christ hasn't changed to divorced, separated, or it's complicated. We have to make sure that we keep up what we did with God before the relationship after we are in the relationship. Continue to pray, fast, read, and worship. It's unfair to God if we forget about Him after we get what we want. Continuing on in those things serves as life insurance. They are going to help you during rough times. Never give up what you know to do just because something new has entered your life. There will be times when you can't turn to your new friend, but you will always have God to depend on. We shouldn't be running back to Him like, *um excuse me God, if you remember me, I'm sorry for leaving you for him, but I really need you right now.* Nah!

Keep God first, it's that simple. If we had to seek him first to get things, how easy will it be for him to start revoking some things if we put Him on the back burner?

When I first started dating in the Kingdom I was so excited. Now mind you, it was a complete difference because now I had to be conscious of my connections and pray and get advice. Before Christ, I talked and dated who I wanted to, for how long I wanted to and it didn't matter. But now my perspective was changed. My first dating experience on this side was a true learning experience. I could see the potential of our relationship and where God could take us together in ministry. All the while I had just received the indwelling of the Holy Spirit. So I had two people in my life that I was getting acquainted with. I would spend a lot of time talking and texting my new boyfriend day after day. We would go to dinner, catch a movie here and there, I mean we really enjoyed each others company. Other people encouraged the relationship and he was ready to settle down with someone in ministry, we thought this could turn out to be a great and prosperous relationship turned marriage. I was so caught up with my new boo that I didn't realize that I was neglecting God, my new found and first love. There were times when my conscious told me that it was time to get off of the phone, not to reply to the text message or that I needed to go home, but I ignored those thoughts.

At a bible study one night, one of our Pastors preached a message titled, *rest for the weary* and she called for an altar call. Before I knew it I was standing at the altar with my saved self. I was still fresh in the Kingdom and recently filled with His Spirit but I had strayed away from seeking God. A leader prayed for me that night and my negligence was confirmed. I had developed a regular regimen with the Lord and it was interrupted by my own agenda. At the altar I was told to seek God how I did when I was seeking the Holy Ghost. I giggled to myself because I remembered how I sought after God. That was some serious seeking! When I was seeking for the Holy Ghost I was determined to receive. I mean every chance I got to praise God in a great atmosphere I took it. One time our women's group traveled to a conference and I was so adamant about receiving the Holy Ghost that I laid at the altar crying out to God long after the people were dismissed from service. The poor little lady that was sitting with me thought I was bound by un-forgiveness and she thought my other friend who came with me for support had a demon. Girl, I just wanted all of God! H quickly things can change. Here I was at another altar crying out having lost that very drive. Although it was only a few months before that I received, I still needed to get back to how I sought after God. God was accustomed to our communion and He needed me to get back to it. Unbeknownst to me, I fell into the common trap of distraction and it was all because I wanted to be in a relationship.

God will get His point across to His people clearly. When we are unable to hear God or when we refuse to hear God when He speaks to us, he will always send a messenger. We will be without excuse. As I was heading home from that eye-opening service I got a surprising meeting from my Pastor. He began to share with me the things that God showed him about me and my decision. That was the first time that God used my leader to tell me directly what was going on in my life and I could not deny the words he spoke.

After that conversation I began to recall every time I ignore those conscious thoughts and that when I realized the conscious thoughts was the Holy Spirit the entire time instructing me. He was showing me the way, He was trying to direct my path but it was as long as I had an ear to hear what He was saying. Now I have an ear to hear. We should desire to be sensitive to the leading of God, especially concerning who we connect ourselves to. We have to be more than careful, we have to be prayerful. Don't ignore that still small voice because you just might miss your exit!

If we were to get technical, God never said anywhere in His word that we would get married. The first command given to man was to dress it and keep it. A mate followed those instructions. Adam was told to be about the business that was placed before him and then God took care of the rest. Companionship followed. This is probably why people have told me that a relationship will come when I least expect it. They say it usually happens when you aren't even looking for it, because it's looking for you. Blessings come when God can trust us with more.

One way that I stay encouraged and motivated in the state that I am in is having confidence in this one thing, "God knows what I can handle". When Adam was in the garden doing whatever he was doing, God looked down from heaven and said that it wasn't good for that guy to be alone. From that point God made the necessary moves to allow a companion to enter Adam's world. For this reason alone, I am encouraged in the hard times of singleness. When it seems like God isn't worried about what I think I need, I know He is fully aware. I know God is looking down on me saying, "I know she can handle this season although she thinks she can't". On top of that He won't put more on me than what I can bear. So apparently He can trust me with this single season. If that wasn't the case I would have been married two times ago.

All in all God has proven Himself many times to be a better life manager than I could ever be. Yes sometimes I wish I could get away with doing things my way, but in the end, my way is never the right way. When my brother graduated from basic training for the Army National Guard, the Drill Sergeant welcomed the soldiers in with a cadence. That was the most entertaining part in the celebration to me. As the soldiers entered, the Drill Sergeant shouted a command and the soldiers shouted back a response. If someone would have tried to do or say their own thing it would have messed up the order of the entire line. The words were, *Just the other day I heard a Drill Sargent say! If you want to be a soldier you gotta do it my way! My way or the Highway! My way or the dog-gone highway! My way's the right way and your way's the wrong way*! I'm telling you, watching the soldiers march synchronized, one by one, flooding into the auditorium was amazing; but when I really thought about what he was saying it reminded me of my walk with Christ. If I want to be a Christian I got to do it His way. There is no other way around doing it God's way. It's His way or the highway and sure enough my way is the wrong way! So we have to keep that in mind. We should want to be pleasing to God in all things and if learning how to encourage ourselves and being content is what it takes then dog-gone-it I'm on it!

Speaking for myself, the problem I have had in the past is jumping out of the boat too early. What that means is I would go for who I thought to be the best thing coming my way, then fall quickly into the trap of distraction. I would do this without getting an understanding of who this person was and why they have come into my life. Do you know that people are sent into our lives for a reason and a season? The person could have been sent my way for me to witness and minister to them, but I done messed around and caught feelings for the assignment. Now my witness is all messed up because I'm googley eyed with butterflies in my stomach. Yes, I'm going to tell the whole truth.

This is where I have been. I have anxiously given out my heart in hopes that the right person will catch it, protect it, and love me back. What I was really doing is spiritually throwing out a fleece, asking if it was God's will. After five failed attempts to play matchmaker in my life I called it quits. Yes, five! Oh no sista-girl, you are all out of tries, no more lives to spare, do not pass go, do not collect two hundred dollars. It was time to seek the Lord.

I felt like Leah. Poor Leah tried her hardest to be loved by a man who tolerated her, but didn't love her as much as he loved another woman. All she wanted was him to pay her some attention and to love her back as she loved him. Some of us women just want to be loved back. Some of us put out a lot of love and expect just a little bit of that in return, and if we don't see the return we will try to provoke it. If we haven't done it we know someone who has. Yes, you know the woman who goes above and beyond to get a man to love her back. We will let them use the car, stay at the apartment free and clear, use up our credit; we will even go as deep as accepting physical, mental and emotional abuse just for his love. We will have child after child thinking he will stay with us. We know her or we are her. We are modern day Leah's. Look at how history repeats itself.

Leah gave Jacob child, after child, after child, until she had an epiphany. She decided that after all of those tries and no proof of love being returned by the man she was connected to, she was going to give it all to God and put Him first. Just like Leah, it was time for Randi to get back to praising God how she used to. It was time to get refocused and time to continue to reach toward the mark of the higher calling. Try after try, and still no result of love in my life. After my Reuben, Simeon and Levi it was time for me to birth my Judah!

Genesis 29:31-35 *And when the LORD saw that Leah [was] hated, he opened her womb: but Rachel [was] barren. And Leah conceived, and bare a son, and she called his name Reuben: for she said, Surely the LORD hath looked upon my affliction; now therefore my husband will love me. And she conceived again, and bare a son; and said, Because the LORD hath heard that I [was] hated, he hath therefore given me this [son] also: and she called his name Simeon. And she conceived again, and bare a son; and said, Now this time will my husband be joined unto me, because I have born him three sons: therefore was his name called Levi. And she conceived again, and bare a son: and she said, Now will I praise the LORD: therefore she called his name Judah; and left bearing.*

The Waiting Room

This is the most critical part in our lives. It's the period of time between where you are and where you are going. How we handle this stage will determine how we spend the rest of our lives once we make it out of the waiting room. Everyone handles this time differently and it's due to perspective. Some get into the waiting room and lose all hope and have a miserable experience. While others find this journey to be precious because they can perfect things in their lives, some just try to pass time because they have the understanding that the waiting room doesn't last forever. Singleness can be for a second or a season. Honestly for me it seems like a really long season, like an entire century, but I am gaining more and more understanding while in it.

In the waiting room some of us will give up on God. This is usually when we find other things to focus on. This is when we forget or forfeit the promises of God for a shortcut. The wait is also when we gain insight, strength, revelation, a greater anointing and deeper understanding of God and ourselves. God is able to manifest himself to us to the fullest because we are alone and it's just you and Him.

Some of us have become so dependent on relationships that when we are without one, it seems like it's the end of the world. I remember a time when I broke up with a guy that I was seeing for a few months and my entire demeanor was different. A close friend of mine brought it to my attention that I wasn't the same old Randi that I was a few days prior. Then I realized that I was so comfortable being with someone that the absence of that relationship brought a damper to my life. If someone walks out of your life today will you be prepared to move forward alone, or will it be rain on your parade?

The waiting room is different for all of us but we must seek God for His guidance. Hannah was a woman who had a waiting room experience. Her life is an example of having a desire for someone, and while you're without and nothing seems to be changing in your own life you have to watch others enjoy their blessings. With that being her life, she managed to get before God to give him her petitions. At that time there was a priest in the temple and when she left her prayer session, the man of God didn't tell her what to do next, she just did it. She left and put herself in a position to receive the blessing in the time it was promised. Sure enough in its appointed time the promise of a son came to fruition.

Let's look at a natural doctor's office waiting room. There are many different things going on in the lives of the visitors. There are people who were there before you, some who came the same time as you, and some who came after. Each person's need to be seen by the doctor varies and the reasoning isn't always disclosed to the onlookers. Depending on a person's need it may cause someone who arrived after you to be seen before you and there is nothing you can do about it, especially if that person had an appointment. How dare we judge another person's visit or get upset because they get called or chosen before we do.

In the waiting room, the office has provided things to make our wait a little more tolerable. There is usually something to drink, read, and a nice comfy seat to relax in. Can you see where I am going with this? In the waiting rooms, we need to recognize the drink that's being offered. God says to come to

Him, all those who thirst and He will give us drink until we are overflowing. An overflow can take our mind off of what's not flowing. Then we need to recognize the good read that's available. We can dive into and dissect the word of God and receive the promises that He has for us. This will take our attention off of what someone else isn't promising us. Lastly, we need to recognize the seat that is before us and take a seat at the feet of Jesus. This is the good part that will not be taken from us. When we take advantage of the time that we have at God's feet in our singleness we gain strength to endure and we enjoy precious moments with God, our husbandman.

Hannah took her desire to God! She didn't run around town telling all the other ladies that she was unfulfilled and not satisfied. Discretion shall preserve you. You do not have to tell everyone that you are struggling in your season, they can't change your situation anyway, so take it to the one who can! Hannah reached a point where it was time for God to move in her life. Either He needed to move or he needed to provide a word of comfort in her time of need. She had an adversary who provoked her, who teased and taunted her, who threw her lack in her face to make her miserable year after year. Have you ever been teased and taunted by the sight of a bragging person? Those people are not sent to push us to depression or jealousy, but to our knees. Do not covet what others have, seek the Lord for what is yours. No one knows the nights you have cried to embrace a relationship. No one knows the nights you have been tormented or tempted to settle for whatever walks through your heart's door. And no one knows the trying times you wanted to give in but you held on. Here's a message to those who are doing the taunting, do yourself a favor and quit while you're ahead because you are only pushing someone closer to their blessing. Oh the day when your enemies see you enjoy your blessing! Rejoice! It's coming!

Psalm 23:5 You prepare a table before me in the presence of my enemies; You anoint my head with oil; My cup runs over.

You can read 1 Samuel 1:9-20 in your leisure. Here is my breakdown of it with added emphasis. Hannah had reached her breaking point and she needed the Lord to work a miracle in her life. She managed to get herself together and make her way to the temple. The temple is wherever you are able to get in the presence of God. It can be your church, car, closet or grocery store aisle. Sometimes we just need to press into His presence. She prayed to God, asking Him to look down on her situation and see what she was going through and to remember her when He was passing out blessings. Her heart was saying "do not forget to stop by my house when you are in the neighborhood answering prayers". On top of the petition she vowed that if He gave her what she was asking for that she wouldn't allow it to replace Him in her life, but she will dedicate it back to Him. Hanah was mature enough to handle the blessing. She understood that every good and perfect gift comes from God; therefore she wouldn't forget Him when He blesses her. We can never get so focused on the blessing that we forget the blessor. That's the right spirit Hannah!

The priest that was in charge of the temple thought she was drunk because she didn't speak a word when she was praying to God, she spoke her request in her heart. That lets me know that people on the outside don't understand our worship. Our praise is misunderstood. We can't expect people to understand what we are pouring out before the Lord. They just need to know that our worship is for real. She told him that she wasn't drunk, but a woman who wanted God to bless her. So he came in agreement with her petition and she went home. When Hannah went away, she ate and her face was no longer sad. Do you see what trusting God to answer prayers will do? It will change your entire countenance. One minute you can be sad and discouraged but when you give it all to God you should gain a confidence that He has heard every spoken and unspoken request.

Here is a great example of walking in faith. After praying, Hannah went home and got with her husband. She started to be the part before the blessing even came her way! She prayed for God to remember her. We normally remember something when we are in a familiar place, or something is similar, or something is brought back to our remembrance due to connections and association. I do it all the time. I can walk into a space and know I was supposed to do something, but unconsciously forgot what it was. My conscious will cause me to remember because that area was a trigger to my memory. I think it went the same way with Hannah. In order for God to remember us, we have to position ourselves in line with what we have petitioned. Disclaimer: putting yourself in position does not mean putting yourself out there, broadcasting that you're lonely and willing, or carrying yourself loosely open for men to pick you up. Keep it clean for the King! Getting in position is simply being about your Father's business and seeking the Kingdom so He can add to you. God will make you known to someone, don't try to be recognized.

Then it came to pass in the process of time that Hannah conceived and bore a son. Hannah had to experience a waiting room but when it was her time, the answer to her prayer came forth! Get your word. Seek God as you know to do and trust that it may not come overnight, it may take a few days, months, or years, but nevertheless it will come to pass.

I admire this story because it depicts a woman waiting on God to answer a prayer. She didn't have a suddenly experience. She was waiting for a child to be born and we know that can take up to nine months, some times longer. Her patience shows us that we can be content when we are waiting on God, because during the process something beautiful is developing.

76

The day of birth makes the wait worth while. Just know that you aren't waiting just to wait, something beneficial is taking place. Let that thing develop so when its time to come forth it's a healthy bundle of joy, free from complications and risk. Which leads me to my next point.

Be the part

My pastor says often that it's not about finding the right person but about being the right person. Ladies we need to be the part before our mate finds us. Just as an actress prepares to go for a leading role, she becomes the part before even getting the casting call. Being a perfect mate is impossible. I believe we can get close to being a perfect match for someone and offer balance and value to our mate, but perfection, no way! We are imperfect people, so we definitely can't expect a flawless relationship when we are paired up with another imperfect person.

How do we "be the part"? Invest in yourself while you are single. Find value in yourself while you are alone. Learn to love who you are. Have you told yourself you were beautiful lately? I remember how I used to walk with my head hung low and a mean mug on my face. I wasn't upset and I wasn't depressed, but I wasn't happy with myself. I would stare in the mirror and pick myself apart with the things that made me a flawed individual. I did that not realizing those were the things that made me that unique individual that I am. When I seen myself I saw a mess; a big nose, skinny legs, big lips, crooked smile, ugly teeth and with each degrading thought I pushed my esteem lower and lower. But I have the understanding now that I was made just how God envisioned me to be. He allowed just enough of my momma's genes to mix with my dad's, and then topped me off with His own special touch. There is no one else like me. There is no one created like you are created. These revelations of ourselves are investments that will be with us forever. Get comfortable with your own skin.

Allow God to reveal who you are in Him. Oh you want to know how to invest into yourself naturally? How about opening up a savings account and actually save! Prioritize and don't splurge at tax season! Add worth to yourself. Find ways to generate revenue. Pay off some of those past due bills and build up your credit. Learn how to cook more than those same four meals, fried chicken, spaghetti, pizza and Hamburger Helper. Ask yourself: am I too busy for a relationship? Am I too mean to love on someone else? Am I messy? Am I immature? Can I clean? Can I really handle the stress of being a wife like I pretend to be? Am I about that life?

I read a quote and it sent me into thought. It read, "While many ladies are trying to find a rich husband, I am trying to be a rich wife". That spoke volumes! Spiritually and naturally I want to be a rich wife. I don't want my husband to be the bread winner alone and become dependent on him. I want to be a blessing too; spiritually, mentally, physically, financially, the whole nine.

The wisest man to ever walk this earth, who had hundreds of women in his time stated that a virtuous woman was a rare creature. He made her seem like an extinct being.

Proverbs 31:10 who can find a virtuous woman? For her worth is far above rubies.

This generation's perception of women has been distorted and it's accepted all over. No one wants to stand against it! It's an epidemic that needs to stop. Every female is claiming to be a bad girl and a five star chick, but what about being a virtuous, God fearing woman? You are considered top notch by how tight your pants are and how much skin is exposed. What's wrong with being a woman who has ambition and has kept herself pure until marriage?

Hey, even if you messed up while in sin or fell into a little sin after Christ, we serve a God who specializes in rededicating things! Rededicate yourself and your body to the Lord and He will keep you!

I want to touch that issue just a little because we have become brainwashed and think that just because we may not have saved ourselves until marriage or we may have had children before we came to Christ that we can no longer live a holy and righteous life. That's a lie from the pit of hell. God can restore! I am a witness of both ends of the stick. When I came to Christ I wasn't married, yet I was wild in the streets and I had a child. God helped me manage the lust of my flesh. I gained an understanding that my body was the temple for the Holy Spirit and that I was not my own. I wanted to please God in every way and if that meant denying my flesh, although at times it seemed impossible, I would do all I could to please God and God only. That's a determining factor to some people when they are considering coming to Christ.

I've been asked how I was able to make the change of not having sex. Even with their puzzled looks, I tell them that it's possible. If keeping myself free from sexual sin is what's going to keep me in line with God, then yes, I will live without it. Was that answer always firm? No. Were there times that at any moment I could have fallen? Yes. That's why the bible says to flee youthful lust because we have to stay aware and away from what triggers our flesh. Our flesh is weak for the things it likes although the Spirit is willing to please God. I am thankful for all of the times God has provided a way of escape even when I backed myself into a corner. If you find yourself in a weak moment, find the way out, because there usually is one. It could be that odd moment when you're seconds away from landing that kiss and the phone rings or suddenly your roommate comes home. Those moments are called divine interventions. Don't be mad, praise God for those!

Another way to be the part is by not letting a man validate your worth. If a man's approval is your only sense of worth, if he was to ever leave you, he will take that validation right on with him, putting you back at square one. Find security within yourself. Be sure and unmovable on your own. An enemy can tear you down with words, but when you have a revelation of who you are those words mean nothing. Use the old saying

the kids say. I'm rubber and you're glue, whatever you say

bounces off of me and sticks to you! Sometimes you got to do

whatever it takes to protect your virtue!

Help I've Fallen

So you have fallen and either someone said or you think you can't get up, right? Wrong! You can get up. That is a lie, the results say satan is using one of his tactics to keep God's people bound by sin, guilt, and shame. In no way shape or form do we have a license to mess up and sin freely, but not having an understanding of repentance, remorse, forgiveness, and grace can paralyze or sentence us to a spiritual death. Be free from bondage of not knowing!

Our God is omniscient, all knowing. He is aware of our fleshly weaknesses and knows what pushes our buttons. Because of His knowledge, if we just so happed to get caught up He usually will send those divine interventions as I mentioned before to give us an escape route. If this does not apply to you that is ok, but the bible warns many times to take heed lest the same thing comes upon you. Please don't be so sure about yourself and your ability to fight off temptation in comparison to your brother or sister. There is nothing good within us, we have a sinful nature. I heard someone say, "we are naughty by nature".

When we hold ourselves on a higher standard in a judgmental way God can easily prove to us that we aren't as strong as we think we are. Ok so if this is where you are, here are three things to help you counteract your adversary. Repent. Get over it. Stay on guard.

Those three things can assist you in your road to recovery. When we repent of our sin we are confessing that what we have done is against God and His will for our life. Might I add that if you have a mind to acknowledge your wrong actions, give praise; because that means somewhere you are a changed person. A sinner isn't aware of their actions being wrong. When I sinned, before I welcomed Christ into my life, I was ignorant to conviction. There wasn't a standard in my life that measured my wrongs. But when I was born again and sinned, that standard, that measure of conviction told me I crossed the line. Conviction pricked my heart and caused me to repent. Only a changed person is conscious to a mistake that's considered normal to others.

Once we have repented and believe that we have received forgiveness for our sin from our heavenly father we have to get over it. Do not dwell on the fact that you messed up. Get up, get dressed and decide that on this brand new day, full of brand new mercies, you are going to take advantage of the newness granted by your Savior. Ask God to keep you from the things that causes you to fall. Ask that He gives you the ability to keep your eyes upon Him and not your own desires. Ask Him to protect you from your emotions.

As women we are emotional beings and we can overthink things and make matters worse just by the chaos that's created by our thoughts. I'm not saying don't think on it as if you didn't do it, I mean don't allow your mind to place you in that situation again with guilt. Have you ever made a mistake and then you began to beat yourself up about it days down the line simply because it crossed your mind again? Sometimes it's a simple thought of the mistake that gets us out of our hook up and now we are thinking, "man I really shouldn't have done that", "I wonder if God has really forgiven me", "I wonder if such-and-such is going to judge me", "why did I have to be so ignorant".

Take authority over the thoughts that are trying to take authority over you! Do not be ignorant to a device of the enemy. Satan doesn't want us to have the victory over sin, so he wants us to wallow in our mistakes. Rise up and declare that you are not defined by your mistakes. If God has forgiven you then accept it and forget about it!

Lastly, we have to stay on guard. You can never get comfortable with sin. If you welcome it in, quickly escort it back out of your life. Stay guarded because you can make the place of issue a familiar place. Sin can be a tad easier the second, third, fourth and fifth time if we have been in that position before and know what it's like. Once we have fallen into sin, it's possible to get over the initial shock of sinning against God. And because we know what to do we can master the art of repenting and bouncing back. This mind state can make it more common for us to mess up again because sin is now familiar. This state is what you want to stay protected against. It should never be easy and comfortable to sin against our God, who is just, righteous, loving and kind. Who also sees and knows all and has the power to stop life at the power of His thought. We should feel convicted and desire to do better.

We can't take His mercy and grace for granted. I repeat, we do not have a license to sin. There is no way to finagle the situation. Do not reason with yourself and believe a lie. Here are some things we can say to ourselves that takes mercy and grace for granted, "Well God you did say you'll forgive me", "the bible says where sin abounds grace much more abound", "God all I have to do is repent". Yes all of those things are true but you are accountable for your actions once you know. Once you know the truth, once you are instructed on how to behave, then it's all on you. Look at the growing pains of a child. There is a difference in the level of punishment when a child is warned the first time around in comparison to the third time. By the third time a child should know better and they must face the consequences whereas they could be pardoned on time one and possibly two. God has mercy and grace but He will not tolerate us falling into sin just because we know that He will forgive us. He also knows that we know better and that we have that mind frame. We cannot outsmart an all knowing God.

To my ladies who are genuinely striving to live holy and righteous before God but you have a few flaws, He knows you too! He still called you and knew you before your issue. He is just awesome like that. He knows where your finish line is. He knew you would struggle and He knew He was going to bring you out. Give Him your hand and let Him pull you out! You have to meet Him half way because He's not going to do all of the work. The hard part, conquering sin, was already done! Just stretch forth your hand. Submit to God, resist the devil and he will flee. That is promised to you. Where we go wrong is not submitting to God first yet still expecting the devil to get off our backs. God needs your cooperation to bring deliverance to your house, you have to want it. You have to be willing to clean it up or eventually you'll go right back to the same mess you were in. It's proven.

Proverbs 26:11 As a dog returns to his own vomit, So a fool repeats his folly.

To the woman who is a habitual faller, get up and stay up! I speak life! Make a definitive decision that pleasing God permanently is more important than gratifying your flesh temporarily.

Math is a tough subject to my daughter. I see her time after time struggling to get answers right even after we do everything to perfect the test. When I see her ready to give in, I encourage her and say, "Baby girl, you have to make the problem work for you so you can get it right. Find an easy way to make it make sense in your head; this will help you get through the problem". It's mental math. I believe ladies; we can apply the same principle when we find ourselves facing a tough and tempting situation. Whether you're close to falling or you have fallen, find a way for victory to make sense in your head. When you do that it helps you get through the problem. Are you still a little unclear?

Randi God is able to keep you. You don't have to make this decision right now. You have been on the right track; God has seen your sacrifice and obedience. Don't get weary! Girl back away from that tree! Step away from that fine man. Don't you think about looking back. Now you know all you have to do is ignore that call and don't reply back to the text. Don't give in!

When we speak life to our situations we are fighting temptation. Sometimes we need to give ourselves a personal pep talk! When no one knows what you are struggling with. When you are battling with a situation and it's critical that no one knows, not even your prayer partner. Speak life and watch God move. No one has to know. When we take the initiative to stand against sin and temptation boldness is given to us. A holy boldness that allows us to stand against things we never thought we'd be able to stand against. Our flesh can lead us into some interesting and compromising situations but if we think before we act, we can avoid a lot of unnecessary fumbling. It means nothing if we think to do well yet reject the very thought and act out in disobedience.

Romans 7:19 For the good that I will to do, I do not do; but the evil I will not to do, that I practice.

The bible is very clear on the fact that the Spirit is willing but the flesh is weak. Our spirit man is rooting for our ability to withstand but flesh is making temptation look

91

irresistible. We have to know what to do in times like this. What will be our final answer? What side will we take? Choose this day!

But Randi, what if I messed up and people know about it? I'm glad you asked because this is another reason to stay guarded. We have to steer clear from the opinions or perspective of others. We have to protect our character. Satan loves to kill our character and he will do this by using people to pollute the air with rumors, assumptions, and lies. But keep your head up high and be about your business. Reputation is who they say you are and character is who you really are. Sometimes when you hear things about yourself laugh because you know it's not who you are and the individuals who matter knows it isn't you as well.

Another way to stay guarded is to be careful of your actions. You have to be sure to not let your good be evil spoken of. I used to hear that phrase all the time and wonder what it meant. It's this simple; don't let it look like you're doing anything wrong. The enemy is seeking whom he may devour and one way he can accomplish that is by ruining your character. You may be able to fly by the radar and God can cover you and your mistake, but if you continue to put yourself in compromising positions, then from the outside looking in you can give affirmation to the assumptions and accusations. All of this can have a major effect on your esteem, confidence or lack thereof. It can also taint your influence.

Don't worry yourself because they "know", because He "knew". Before the foundation of the world was form He knew your ending! A person can judge you on this earth for your human nature, but God has the final say. I've heard the stories of Pastors and leaders putting people on blast if they fall into sin and people being openly rebuked for things they have done. Don't get me wrong, there is a place and a time to handle protocol if it's with cause, but ultimately what's done in the dark is seen and judged by God. If it isn't God instructed, leaders can do more damage to a person by putting their business out. God is the judge and forgiver of unrighteousness and I believe He wants to protect His name so He protects His people from being exposed if it's unnecessary. Let's take a look at Mary, although she was without sin, her situation is a perfect example. Mary was a virgin but one day found out she was pregnant. Oh goodness, what a revelation that would be to some of us! When her husband found out the news he wanted to divorce her and keep her hidden because it was an embarrassment. But the bible states, *he didn't want to make her a public example*, and another translation says *he didn't want to expose her to public disgrace* which would have come by him exposing her. The point is people need to be led by God if or when they expose a person's sin. We have to leave room for God, who can deal with a person in personal times and cause them to repent for their wrong without being made a public spectacle.

God and God only have we sinned against. So what if others find out? God knew first. But if you are blatantly falling into sin and bringing reproach upon your ministry, position, and or character then you need to humble yourself and take a sit down. There is a difference between the person with a real issue and the person who's fully aware of their wrong actions.

If you happen to get wind of some juicy information of a fallen person, don't be the one to spread it. Uplift them in prayer and consider yourself! If you are privileged to know something private about someone, it's your responsibility to pray for them and not run and tell that! I should be comfortable and know that if God show you anything about Randi B. I am being covered and not being exploited in the tabloids! If you are the fallen, be willing to stop and get back on track. No need for baby steps, just do it. Don't answer, don't call, don't hook up, don't entertain and don't think you are stronger to go back into a familiar situation without the help of God.

Satan wants to imprison us by getting us to believe that if or when we mess up God isn't going to forgive us. Sooner or later if you feed into the lie you'll start to agree with it and live it. So the moment you start to believe that you might as well continue in sin. "The devil is a lie and his breath stinks" as I heard a Pastor say. A just man falls, but the amazing part of the scripture is that he gets back up. This is the advantage of being a child of God and having a revelation of God's unchanging love.

He loves you and He doesn't want you to live in bondage.

Repent, get over it, and stay guarded!

Desperate

Desperate times calls for desperate measures! This may not be a problem for you, but again, when the time clock is ticking and we feel like we are getting too old, too fat, or too impatient, we can end up making a man out of dirt and that is God's job. It's easy to think that if you get with any man God will work on him because you two are together and God just works backwards like that. Girl, let go and let God! I've noticed that us single girls are willing to jeopardize our relationship with God for a natural relationship. That is a trick of the enemy. Let him go and don't be afraid to do so. What is the saying? If it's meant to be it will all come back to you. It's easier for someone to pull you down than for you to pull them up. So be careful what you set your affections on.

Desperate measures come from being love struck or love stuck for the sake of understanding the seriousness of the matter. This is a dangerous place. I've witnessed and experienced disobedience from being love stuck and boy crazy. The only way to avoid or get out of this is to keep our love for Christ first and above all other loves. I was boy crazy at one point. I was hopelessly stuck and I couldn't even recognize what was happening to me. I was able to joke with a friend of mine after the fact by saying that I was like a child when it came to relationships. When I have a crush on a person, I really like them. Emotionally I can go from one to ten very quickly. Sometimes it seemed as if it was overnight. It has taken me years to really put this issue in perspective and learn how to counteract those feelings. That behavior was setting me up to fail. It was as if I didn't have self-control, which is why I depend on the help of the Holy Ghost now. It felt like I was giving out my love bit by bit, in hopes that someone would feel the same way towards me. But I was left alone to deal with all of my emotions. This has caused me to guard my heart. When I love, I love hard, not realizing that the mentalities of those I was interested in were far from settling down. After so long that tampered with my self-esteem and self-worth. I began to think that I was the problem.

Back to the boy craziness. Because I am such a thinker, there was a time when I entertained the thought of a relationship with a person, which then led to us hooking up shortly after.

Things quickly began to pick up; phone calls and long conversations, text messages all through the day, lunch, dinner dates, movie nights, laughs and gifts. It wasn't long before the infamous words, I love you appeared on the scene. With all of those gestures, in the back of my mind I still hoped that this was the one. But wait! I was so involved and dazed at my awesome relationship that I ignored some important factors. Instead of worrying about how much he thought I was wifey material, I should have been making sure our lives were lined up to God's will. I was excited and falling in love with who he was going to be. I seen his potential and because I was so love struck I wasn't even helping him actually get there. The potential is what captured me and that's only who he's capable of being or becoming. It wasn't guaranteed. He wasn't even what I seen he could be yet. The crazy part is I don't know if he even seen his potential.

The problem wouldn't have been in our dating, it would have come after we said "I do". I would have woke up the next morning asking who this person was that I joined myself to. "Wait a minute; you aren't the person that's supposed to be here.

You aren't the one I was expecting to be with. Where is the guy that I dreamt about and woke up thinking about? Oh wait it was all my imagination." Dun, Dun, Dun! The moment of truth was I never let him get there. It was a smooth crash, head first into reality.

Me accepting his *not yet* could have caused him to never reach the potential that I knew he could reach. I needed to leave room for God and I failed to do that. Accepting him as he was and not encouraging him to progress would have birthed complacency. He would have taken on the mentality, "oh she gone take me as I am. No car, no job, no goals, cool!" and many of us settle for that. We are ok because in the end we can say that we got a man. I don't want to be her. You shouldn't be her either. We can accept them, for who they are, but our love for them shouldn't allow them to stay where they are. This applies to everyone we are connected to.

Don't settle for the unfinished product. We should want the man God has worked on and made ready. Just as we have prepared ourselves we should desire someone who has prepared also.

100

But I've been waiting for a long time and Mr. Random-Guy seems to be the only one interested in me. As long as I still have breath in my body, I'd rather wait on an answer from God in a moment than be miserable for a lifetime because of impatience. All of this puts me in the mind frame of an auto auction. Let's say I need a car bad! Because of my many bad judgments and experiences with automobiles I have to have wisdom and patience to not jump at the first car coming by. If I put my bets in on the first thing that looks and sounds good, I could miss out on the better selections a little later, the ones no one wanted to wait for. Sometimes the wait is worth it. Does that mean your blessing isn't right in front of you? No! This is why you have to seek the Lord for your direction. Your sister a few rows over may get blessed with a mate immediately while you're continually ripping the calendar sheets off and counting the months since your last date. Everyone's journey is unique. It's a dangerous combination to be lonely, weak, and desperate. Not weak physically, but weak in waiting. Do you remember I said God doesn't set us up to fail him we do that all by ourselves? With that knowledge we have to take precaution and heed the warning signs of things that are coming to get us to fall in a lonely, weak, and desperate state. The saying is true, *when you play with fire you get burned*. It may seem like the attack of attraction and temptation is at an all-time high in certain seasons, but be strong and wise enough to not entertain anything that has the ability to take you out. It's your responsibility to know your limits and what God is saying don't touch, don't talk to and don't open. Be confident that satan knows what you like but God knows what u need.

As women of virtue, we shouldn't be so quick to jump the broom with any Joe Schmoe, especially when we weigh out the time invested into our lives. Take your time; you'll have the rest of your lives together. There's no redo with the "I do". When we give ourselves away, we give away the precious treasure that God has dug out and it's priceless. Don't throw your pearls to the swine girl!

Celebrate others

Invitation after invitation, bridal shower after engagement party, dress shopping and smiles, but yet it's all for your friends and family. Have you been there? Congratulating and wishing the best of luck, and helping send thank you notes are the things that have consumed your life. Well at least that's what it seems like. Isn't it funny how one moment you're doing fine dealing with being single, but then a season of festivities comes along and stirs up your emotional pot. Now you're frustrated because it is not your day. It seems like everyone else is getting blessed, but you. We are almost to the end, go ahead and tell the truth. *Wink!*

It can be very easy to slip into a state of frustration or bitterness when we judge other relationships to our own. A lot of times we are not frustrated in an envious or covetous manner, it's simply the fact that we haven't experienced this relational bliss we so desire. I mean Cupid, are you out of arrows? As we smile and bid farewells to the newlyweds, I find it interesting that there are many married individuals that think the singles are the blessed ones. So come on now, that should tell us something. If I'm being told, by those who are walking down a path that I desire to one day walk down, to take advantage of this time, don't neglect my singleness, live it up, and so on, I should take heed and be content until it's my time to get to the next stage. They must know something that we don't. The grass isn't always greener on the married side. There's still some work that needs to be put in and personal troubles don't roll away.

Remember I mentioned earlier that some people have different needs and we cannot judge how God decides to move in their lives? That understanding is going to allow us to rejoice with others and celebrate their life advancements. We can't be a fair judge because we don't know how they have spent time in prayer or waiting, just like we are. We can sit all day long stating what we see on the outside, "They just got engaged", "They just got saved", "How did she get a boyfriend?". Those thoughts become a stumbling block for our own blessings. Don't complain because God has a blessing for you too. Sometimes it could be a test. He just may want to see you celebrate and rejoice with your sister or friend. I do believe that when we celebrate with each other without reservation we are operating in a pure

heart. And the bible says:

Matthew 5:8. Blessed are the pure in heart: for they shall see God.

One way we see God naturally is when He moves and

bless our lives. Lord I want to see you, I won't hate, I'll

congratulate.

Outro

I don't want to be comfortable or naive to think that every man who walks into my life is my husband. I need to discern why each person is in my life. If you can relate, ask God for wisdom and discernment to know why people are in your life. The Samaritan woman at the well had five previous relationships before her encounter with Christ. When I read that story it reminded me of myself. When I was honest with myself, I was in a position to get my issue fixed. A wise man said "God can't fix what we can't face". When the Samaritan woman replied truthfully to Christ about her relationship status, God was able to bless her. Trying to pretend like we have it all together will cause us to miss what God wants to do in our life. Christ has the ability to redirect our focus from human companionship to a Godly relationship.

I don't have all of the answers and I haven't perfected this walk, but I wanted to give you my heart. After reading this you may have realized your struggle may not be such a struggle after all. Take what I have spoken and apply what's needed for your walk. I accept the fact that it may have taken me longer to welcome my singleness than what was intended, but I made it. I made it to the point where I can proudly say I am saved, single, and sane. Did you think I was going to say satisfied? I have learned to be content in whatever state I am in, but I'll always desire to seek fulfillment of His will.

During your personal time of solitude, don't blame God or become bitter because a man hasn't come to sweep you off your feet yet. God is still able to keep you. I hope you were encouraged by this message and I pray you have a different outlook. Give God praise because at least you are making it!

I want to hear from you! If you are single, have experienced some interesting things or want to share your lessons learned during your season, contact me! Let's encourage each other! Send any correspondences to msrandi.b@gmail.com.

God bless you! Stay strong.

Psalm 84:11 No good thing does he withhold from those who walk uprightly.

Proverbs 3:6 Trust in the Lord with all your heart, And lean not on your own understanding; In all your ways acknowledge Him, And He shall direct your paths.

My prayer and praise for us

Lord I thank you for every time I tried to go ahead of your plan and you managed to stop me. Thank you for every blessing in disguise, even when I thought you were withholding things from me. Thank you for every open door and every closed door. Thank you for keeping me in my right mind when I thought I was going to lose it. Thank you for keeping me when I wanted to give in. Thank you for convicting me and for forgiving me of every short coming. Thank you for letting me know I am not perfect but Your Spirit is perfecting me. Thank you for not giving up on me. Thank you for loving me, for showering me with your loving kindness, grace and mercy. Thank you for all that you have done and will do. Thank you for putting up with my questions, doubts and fears. Thank you for being my God.

Now Lord, I pray that you will bless every woman that is experiencing a season of solitude. Anoint her in a special way. Father I know each person's experience, struggles and needs are different, therefore, tailor make their help. Reveal to them who You are, who they are and what You are doing in them and for them. Comfort, strengthen, and equip them for their time of waiting. Keep their feet from falling and moving outside of Your will. I come in agreement with every petition they have. I pray they will remember the words that were ministered. I declare she is steadfast and unmovable. I declare she is bold and confident. I declare she is ready to work in the Kingdom. I decree that she's aware of her worth and Your love towards her. What doesn't kill us makes us stronger. Thank you for her sanity.